THE
# NLP
# BUSINESS SIMPLE

## The Stuff You Wish You'd Known Sooner

## By Tracey Baum

# Table of Contents

Dedication ............................................. 5

Foreword............................................... 6

Introduction......................................... 8

Who Is This Book For?..................... 12

How To Use This Book..................... 14

Introduction To Neuro Linguistic
Programming (NLP)........................... 16

Communication That Connects ..... 19

Language Patterns That Influence.. 35

Understanding How People Think... 51

Managing Your Own Mindset......... 67

Selling Without Selling..................... 84

Decision Making That Works........ 101

# Dedication

To Mum who instilled her love
of books and reading into me.

I miss you every day.

# Foreword

This Little Book Of NLP That Makes Business Simple is an absolute gem. Whilst NLP is relatively new, there is now an abundance of books on the subject, varying in complexity and perspective, so where do you start to understand it? Well, the answer is right in front of you, here in this little book.

Tracey has a real talent for breaking down the different topics into accessible language and practical tips. As a Master Trainer of NLP, she has years of experience of teaching practitioners how to apply NLP thinking and explaining how to use this modality. And now she has translated her easy training style onto the page in this Little NLP book.

What makes this book stand apart from others as an initial primer is the translation of theory into practice, so right from the start you can use the tips in different contexts within your everyday life and work. The 15 tips from each I wish I had them at my fingertips when I was starting my NLP learning journey.

Thank you Tracey for a great little book – I will keep it by my side for years to come.

*Gill McKay, NLP Master Practitioner, Sobriety Mentor and Educator*

# Introduction

I started my NLP journey 11 years ago. At the outset, I wasn't sure how I was going to integrate my new learnings into the business I was planning on setting up. I was already a counsellor and alongside my NLP training, a certified hypnotherapist, but NLP, although interesting, was shrouded in complicated ideas and language, and not something I could easily see how it would fit in, or so I thought back then.

Like anything, some things need more time to settle and to percolate. NLP was that for me. The more

I learned, the more I studied and the more qualifications I got, I came to see what a useful tool NLP can be. Now as a Master NLP practitioner and Trainer of NLP, I cannot imagine not using NLP in my business. All my training courses, my workshops and my coaching style incorporate NLP to a huge extent.

NLP has helped me in both my personal and professional life in building and maintaining relationships, understanding how others see the world especially when it's different to mine, using my language carefully to get the best result out of every interaction that I can, understanding the intricacies of our non-verbal communications and using all these techniques to create the world I want to have.

I wanted to write this book for varied reasons. First, NLP has become a passion of mine and I wanted to introduce it to more people without having to spend thousands on a practitioner course. Second, I wanted to introduce it in a way that was easy to understand, removing the jargon and the mystic that surrounds it. Third, I've always wanted to write a book. There's another in the works as well, this time taking the ideas and topics raised in this one and going into a lot more detail. Still though, easily accessible and easy to understand but done for business owners who want to dive deeper into the world of NLP.

I hope you enjoy the book as much as I did writing it.

*Tracey*

# Who Is This Book For?

You're a business owner, maybe you run your business on your own, you might have a small to medium business employing up to 250 people or perhaps you're a big player, running a large corporation type.

Whichever one you're involved in, I know it's not an easy juggling act to master. The bottom line is profit and viability, right? There's nailing communication between both your service users and your staff (if you have them), to marketing your business with the reliability of your brands' values that will attract your ideal employees and a constant source of customers, to adopting the mindset of being achievers and succeeders and finally to making those consistent sales that WILL make your business profitable and viable.

Neuro Linguistic Programming - NLP can be used effectively to provide a structure and methodology that allows you to navigate through these issues. By presenting a toolkit to help you negotiate the obstacle course that running a successful business can throw up, the tips provided here allow you to overcome these hurdles in a way that makes it effective and easier.

# How To Use This Book

The book is split into 6 sections with each section having 15 tips for you to use. Start from the beginning and work your way through each section in order or turn to a section that interests you and dive into that. Or you could be adventurous and daring and open a page, any page, and see what you get.

The sections are as follows:

Communication That Connects

Language Patterns That Influence

Understanding How People Think

Managing Your Own Mindset

Selling Without Selling

Decision Making That Works

# Introduction To Neuro Linguistic Programming (NLP)

NLP is relatively new talking 'therapy'. Devised in the 1970s by Richard Bandler and John Grinder. Simply, they were looking at why some people succeeded in life / business when others seemed to struggle. They observed several therapists as to why their models worked better and from those observations produced their model for success that we call NLP.

They based this on 'an attitude and a methodology that leaves behind a trail of techniques'. The attitude being referred to is that of curiosity, a 'how do they do that?' attitude or a 'how do I do that?' From this, they based their whole ethos on 'modelling' which again in its simplistic terms means, if someone has done something and excelled at it, anyone can. You only need to copy who or what has worked so well and incorporate it into your endeavours.

**Neuro** (our nervous systems) - Relates to how we use our senses to interpret, understand and interact with the world we live in.

**Linguistic** - How we use language both verbal and non- verbal to express ourselves and to communicate to others.

**Programming** - This relates to our mental and behavioural patterns that we use daily. Think habits, traditions and customs here.

# Communication
# That Connects

*You're Always Communicating Something To Somebody*

Our non-verbal body language is our primary way of communicating with others. 93% of the way we communicate is non-verbally. That stat is broken down between body language and voice tone leaving only 7% for the actual words we speak to be heard. Are you always aware of what your body or voice tone is conveying?

Build rapport, build more rapport and then continue to build rapport. It takes a long time to gain this with people and a second to break it. Never underestimate its value.

Maintain eye contact and smile often. This is the universal signal for friend and someone who can be trusted (Be mindful of those with Autism Spectrum Disorders where eye contact is difficult or impossible).

Read the room. What approach will get you the best result from any interaction? How are the people involved looking? Upbeat, energised or tired and lethargic? Is a sympathetic tone or a gung-ho conversation going to get you what you want?

Match the energy being used
in any meetings, networking or
conversations. When you
match someone else's energy,
conversations flow more easily.

Avoid fidgeting. Tapping your foot or fingers, playing with a pen - whatever it might be - tells the other person / people you're a) not feeling confident here or b) you're bored.

Use silences to your advantage.
A well-placed pause, especially
immediately before you do or say
something important, means
instinctively others pay more
attention.

People will always remember how you made them feel over what you said. Particularly with your service users, focus on making them feel valued and happy.

Talk like a human being.
Avoid your business jargon.
Make concepts and ideas simple.
Avoid the use of scripts and keep
your language natural and
conversational.

Match your words to your tone. Ever heard someone say 'I'm fine' but their body language was saying the opposite? **HOW** you say something matters.

Mirror and match people you interact with. Subtly (don't take the P), mirror (copy) and match their posture, pace of speech and language patterns (NEVER accents).

Ask questions that make people think. How is that for you will get a different and truer response than do you understand? This evokes real engagement with people.

Learn to actively listen. This means them talking and not you. Don't interrupt someone part way through what they're saying. Show positive body language like head nodding to encourage them.

Be clear and concise about what you want. Vagueness leads to miscommunication and disappointment. Instead of 'let's connect soon', try 'let's book a call for … day'.

Use stories as often as you can. People remember stories, particularly those that make us laugh or cry.

Know what you want before you speak / interact. If you feel confident about what your outcome is then you will stay focused and on track.

# Language Patterns That Influence

*The Meaning of Communication Is The Response You Get*

As only 7% of how we communicate is verbal, it's important to make that small amount count. I'm sure we've all heard of the idiom, 'words can hurt' but there's also the opposite, "One kind word can change someone's entire day." - Unknown. Understanding how to use language to make an impact and have influence is truly life changing.

Everyone likes to feel they have control in life so provide choices for them. You can ask 'Do you want to sign up for this now?' or 'would you prefer to start this week or next?' The 2nd option makes them feel in charge and you're more likely to get a sign up.

Avoid the 'if' word and replace it with 'when'. **When** plants the idea that something is going to happen and removes any doubt.

Always make it about them, not you. You can be the best at what you do, but what they're wanting to hear is what's the benefit to them.

Remove weak language.
Eradicate the maybes, hopefullys,
justs and onlys from business
conversations. Be confident
in your approaches.

'Because' is a magic word.
More people will come on board
more easily when they understand
why something is needed.
It provides credibility.

Use their language back at them, don't try and use terms you prefer. It's irrelevant if it isn't the way you'd say it. Using their language back shows you've understood them and is a great way at building rapport.

'Imagine' is another key word to sprinkle in regularly. 'Imagine how you'll feel when this project is finished' creates a reality they can then make happen.

Turn **'buts'** into **'and'**.' I see
your point but….' Can appear to
pre-empt conflict or an argument.
'I can see your point AND here's a
different way to look at it..' invites
the conversation to continue
and expand.

Use the power of the people to provide a sense of normalcy. 'Lots struggle with this at first, but then it clicks and they get it'. This reassurance builds trust.

Make the unfamiliar sound familiar. Compare new ideas with concepts they already know. This helps them accept the new idea quicker.

'Yet'. Another word with limitless potential. Using this when overcoming objections minimises the doubt and fear people experience. 'I'm not good at that' is a statement. 'I'm not good at that yet' opens the door for further exploration and progress.

People remember the last thing you say to them. End meetings or conversations on a strong confident note.

Change 'I have to..' into 'I get to...'.
One is a chore; the other is
something potentially exciting.
Changing the energy of words
creates a different impact.

Keep questions open ended. 'Can you?.. invites a yes or no response. Why, where, who, what, when ensures there's a dialogue which diverts the focus on to something more positive.

Using key words and phrases repeatedly allows for these to become entrenched in someone's mind. This is beneficial when you want them to remember and act on aspects of the business.

# Understanding How People Think

## *The Mind and Body Are Connected*

To get yourself or your team motivated and productive, and to attract more customers, understanding what makes them tick is imperative. Once you know this, you can target your approach to elicit the best out of them. Turn weaker points into strengths and grow their existing talents, turning them into superpowers. Imagine what that would do for your business?

Uncover their belief and value systems. What is true to them and what is important. This is the ONE point you MUST know if you want to understand someone.

Know whether you /they are more visual, auditory or rely on how something feels and adapt your language to reflect this. 'I see what you mean' or 'that sounds good' or 'I get where you're coming from'.

Remember some people want the big picture, others want all the little details. Start off big and provide more detail if they ask.

Emotion beats logic. Find their emotional hook and tap into it.

We all process at different speeds.
Deep thinkers need more time.
Avoid rushing into asking for
instant decisions.

Know their time focus. Do they talk and make decisions based on what's been before, what's happening now or how they see things in the future. Listen for clues and talk to them in their time frame.

Ask the right questions.
Delve deep.

People know how *they* make decisions. Some need proof of concept, others to read reviews and some on a gut feeling. Give them what they need.

The first objection is rarely
the real one. Keep digging down,
understand more about them and
you'll find the real reason.

Being understood to most is more important than being right. If someone believes you get them, they'll be more inclined to trust you even when there's a difference in opinions.

Understand their why.
What makes them tick?
This is key to aid motivation.

Certainty is comforting, change is scary. Better the devil you know and all that. Make innovative ideas familiar and safe before implementation.

Embrace their uniqueness.
We like to be seen as individuals
and not lumped in with the masses.
Make them feel special.

Create a safe environment where honesty and sharing are encouraged. We trust when we feel safe before we reveal some of the deeper level stuff.

Flip the narrative when necessary.
Put something into a different
context to get a different
perspective.

# Managing Your Own Mindset

*I Think, Therefore I Am*

In NLP, a mindset is a set of filters, with attitudes and beliefs that form a state (=condition). The mindset in part determines how an individual will respond to situations around them.

We will all face challenges, both professional and personal, throughout our lives - some harder than others - and it is our mindsets that decide how we navigate through these times.

Having a negative mindset keeps us stuck in a never-ending loop, whilst a positive one will propel us through to the other side. Things like perfectionism, imposter syndrome and comparisonitis are examples of a negative mindset, while gratitude, hope and optimism are examples of positive ones.

Your brain believes what you tell it. Feed it rubbish and it will devour it. Feed it well and see what happens.

Control what you can control and don't sweat the other stuff. If it's something you cannot change, stop worrying about it. Focus on what you CAN do.

Confidence isn't a feeling,
it's a decision. We don't wait
to feel confident before we do
something. We act and
confidence will follow.

Act 'As If'. Adopt a posture,
thought process, language pattern
that fits how you would like to
be and it soon becomes
second nature.

Stress is normal. Instead of letting stress inhibit you, change the words attached to it. Replace the word anxiety and try using excited. Note the change in your thinking.

Remove failure from your vocabulary. Take the feedback from your attempt and have another go. The only mistakes are the ones we don't learn from.

Your inner voice is a jerk; the one that tells you you're not good enough, or whatever. If your inner voice is your biggest critic you can choose to ignore it.

Small wins lead to momentum. Don't try and climb Everest before you've had a climbing lesson! Motivation comes from progress. Start with something small and manageable and go from there.

Surround yourself with supporters, not naysayers. If you're constantly around negative people, you'll absorb their energy. Put yourself with those who love, support and push you.

Perfectionism is fear in a fancy outfit. Waiting for everything to be perfect is a great way of avoiding taking any action. Done is better than perfect.

Your brain looks for what you focus on. Ever noticed that when you're thinking of buying a car how suddenly that car is everywhere? It's the same with opportunities. Focus on problems and you'll find them. Focus on solutions and guess what happens?

One bad hour doesn't make a bad day. Stop, breathe and reset. You're in control of how the rest of it goes.

Comfort zones aren't made
of bricks and mortar. They are
moveable. Try leaning on yours a
little and see what happens
when you stretch it.

Your energy and attitudes are your responsibility. Take ownership of how you think and feel and don't let others take that power from you.

Confidence comes from
keeping promises to yourself.
Every time you say you'll do
something and you actually do it,
you build trust in yourself. That's
how confidence grows.

# Selling Without Selling

*Resistance Is A Sign Of A Lack Of Rapport*

There is only one given when running a business of any size. Without sales, there is no business. Anyone in business who isn't selling doesn't have a business, they have a hobby.

For many, the concept of selling is off-putting and the experience of being sold to unpleasant. This is one of the biggest areas I see people struggle with, no matter the size of their enterprise, and this, of course, has a major impact on their profit margins.

There are ways of making this more enjoyable and profitable, both for those doing it and those on the receiving end.

You're not selling a product
or a service. You're solving a
problem. You're selling solutions.
Focus on that.

Not every customer will respond similarly to a single tactic. Having a variety of strategies will help you earn sales from multiple people and grow your business.

Remember it's a conversation.
Eliminate the word 'pitch'
from your thinking.

People buy what they want, not what they need. Get them emotionally invested.

Stop talking. The conversation ratio is 20% you, 80% them. Know when silence is your biggest advantage.

There are 4 main buying patterns: those who buy impulsively, especially if there's an early bird; those who leave it to the last minute; those who are heavily swayed by stats and evidence; and those who buy according to reviews and testimonials.

Make it all about the value
provided, not about the cost.

Avoid being seen as one of those pushy types. This includes aggressive follow ups. Give people time and space.

Be prepared to manage any objection. Understand their perspective and discuss it. Never argue with a prospect. No doesn't always mean never.

Create FOMO. People often want what others have. Instead of 'you should do this..' try, 'most people in your situation choose this ..'

Using stories helps to make the emotional connection and keeps building rapport.

Do your homework. Know your buyer. Check their social media and websites. This helps tailor your approach directly at them.

Make sure you're in conversation with, and building a relationship with, the decision maker as well as any other contact you have.

Be Bold. Sometimes asking, 'is this something you're interested in?', works. As my awesome coach, Taz Thornton often says, 'I'd really love to work with you, I know I can help you with.. .so how about it?'

Here are questions that help with those sales conversations:

What's the biggest issue you have right now?

How do those issues affect you?

What have you already tried to resolve this?

What effect did that have?

What would be your ideal solution?

What is the timescale for this?

# Decision Making
# That Works

*The Person With The Most Flexibility Controls The System*

When you make clear, confident decisions, everything in your business flows better. You save time, reduce stress and stop second guessing yourself, bouncing between ideas but going nowhere.

Clarity also provides your customers and team members with a sense of control and confidence in your brand.

Good decision-making builds momentum. Making bad ones or none at all, costs money, creates confusion and kills progress.

It's not about being 100% right 100% of the time, it's about moving forward, learning as you go, reviewing and adjusting as necessary and keeping that energy going.

Work smarter not harder.
Focus on what affects 80% of the
business. The smaller stuff
comes later.

Who's good at what? If you have a team, who is the best person for the task? If you're a sole trader, who can you outsource to?

Write it down. Keeping things in your head confuses the issue. Put it on paper or mind map on a whiteboard with others.

Cut through overthinking by breaking big decisions into smaller, more manageable steps.

Ask better questions to pinpoint the main driver. 'What's the simplest next step?' is preferable to 'where do I go now?'.

Look for opportunities not obstacles. Use a different perspective to see the issue from another angle.

Understand you may have an unconscious bias. Our brains filter information based on past experiences. That doesn't make them right.

Become a time traveller.
Project yourself a month, 3
months, a year after the decision
has been made. Does it feel right
still? Are you getting the results
you want? If not, adjust.

Get into the right mindset.
If you're tired or stressed you're
more likely to make the
wrong choices.

It's never going to be 100% right.
Settle for 70% and trust
your instincts.